HISTORY OF THE DEFENSE BATTALION

The United States Marine Corps (USMC) has a long history of seizing and

defending advance bases. Prior to World War I, base defense was the Marine Corps'

main mission.[1] During World War I, the Advance Base Force was created to seize and

defend enemy territory, primarily bases. In 1933, the Advance Base Force transformed

into the Fleet Marine Force (FMF) under Commandant Major General Ben Fuller.[2] By

1939, the looming threat of Japanese aggression in the Pacific solidified the need for

advance base defense and Commandant Major General Thomas Holcomb formed four

Defense Battalions to defend advance naval bases from ground and air attack.[3] The core

of the original battalions were formed from two infantry battalions, 1st and 2nd Battalion,

15th Marine Regiment.[4] Subsequent Defense Battalions were formed with air defense

personnel and artillerymen; infantrymen were attached as required. The first Defense

Battalions included nearly 900 Marines, three anti-aircraft batteries, three seacoast

batteries, and ground and anti-aircraft machine gun batteries.[5] Follow on evolutions

included more sophisticated artillery, anti-aircraft guns and search radars. These Defense

Battalions provided the first combined arms teams and proved to be very effective

fighting forces.

By December 1941, Defense Battalions (now totaling six and comprising 5,000

Marines and 20% of the total FMF) defended the islands of Wake, Johnston, and

Midway.[6] Defense Battalions were employed using a detachment concept; task

organizing the force as required for the mission on each island. The remnants of the

deployed units remained at Hawaii for training, recovery, and relaxation. These deployed

Defense Battalions served as the first line of defense against the Japanese. On Midway

Island, First Lieutenant George H. Cannon of the 6th Defense Battalion earned the war's first Medal of Honor on December 7, 1941.[7] Severe Japanese shelling wounded Cannon and he refused to evacuate his post until other wounded Marines evacuated first. He later died from his wounds.

The first Defense Battalions formed in 1939 lacked equipment and infantry for executing counter-attacks. In the spring of 1941, Secretary of the Navy Frank Knox approved the creation of separate infantry battalions to serve with the Defense Battalions in response to growing concern that Defense Battalions could not repel a major hostile amphibious landing.[8] However, the attack on Pearl Harbor and the United States' subsequent entry into the war created more demand for infantry units elsewhere and the Defense Battalions only occasionally received infantry support.[9] Therefore, every Marine in a Defense Battalion also trained to fight as an infantryman.[10] It was beneficial for Defense Battalion Marines to receive this cross-training, however, due to the air threat, Defense Battalion Marines were unable to simultaneously serve as air defenders and infantrymen. On Wake Island, the lack of a counter-attack force was a contributing factor of the outcome of the battle. The detachment on Wake had only 400 men, no radar or sound ranging equipment, and no infantry for a counter-attack.[11] Additionally, the detachment had only 30% (18 of 60) of its allotted .50 caliber machine guns.[12] Despite its shortcomings, the detachment on Wake fought bravely and managed to fend off the Japanese for 15 days, sinking one warship and killing hundreds of Japanese as they came ashore, before finally surrendering on December 23, 1941.[13] A dedicated infantry unit in support of the Defense Battalion may have changed the outcome of the battle.

As the war progressed, the Marine Corps executed more offensive missions and its focus shifted from solely defending bases to seizing and defending enemy islands. The switch to a more offensive employment method of seizing opposed islands forced the Defense Battalions to adapt, and they grew in strength, weaponry, and capabilities. In subsequent assaults, Defense Battalions landed with initial assault waves of the amphibious force and protected the beachheads, harbors, and airfields, thereby freeing infantry units to conduct more offensive missions.[14] At Guadalcanal on 7 August 1942, the 3d Defense Battalion landed amongst the first waves of the 1st Marine Division to defend the beachhead.[15] After Henderson Airfield was secured, the Defense Battalion employed as perimeter security and repulsed several counter-attacks.[16] At Rendova and Guam the Defense Battalions supported the infantry; providing fire support during the assault and then patrolling for remaining Japanese pockets of resistance.[17] By the end of 1943, the Defense Battalions reached a top strength of 19 Battalions comprising 26,685 Marines.[18] As the threat to advance naval bases decreased later in the war, Defense Battalions disbanded or reformed as anti-aircraft battalions, the forefather of today's modern air defense battalions.

Overall, Defense Battalions provided a flexible, combined arms team that proved to be an effective fighting force capable of supporting offensive operations, defending bases from air and ground attack, and conducting secondary infantry missions. Defense Battalions frequently relieved infantry units of defensive missions, such as defending an airfield or a harbor; thereby, freeing the infantry to conduct other missions. Likewise, when the threat dictated, the infantry supported the Defense Battalions in the execution of its mission. Defense Battalions' success during World War II can be attributed to its multi-use weapons, cross trained personnel, and flexibility to execute multi-missions.

Today's two remaining air defense battalions in the Marine Corps conduct similar missions to the Defense Battalions of World War II, defending critical Marine-Air Ground Task Force (MAGTF) assets from ground and air attack. However, they cannot conduct air and ground defense simultaneously due to manpower and equipment shortfalls. A well trained, properly equipped defense unit will be required for the foreseeable future, due to the rapidly evolving unmanned aircraft and cruise missile threat and the necessity to employ land based aviation assets from a forward operating base (FOB) during expeditionary operations ashore, therefore, the Marine Corps should convert Low Altitude Air Defense (LAAD) Battalions into Defense Battalions to provide its air defense and air base ground defense.

THE CURRENT GROUND BASED AIR DEFENSE SITUATION IN THE USMC

Since World War II, air defense units in the Marine Corps have changed significantly. Around 1960, air defense units moved from the Marine division to the Marine Aircraft Wing (MAW), as surface to air missiles replaced anti-aircraft guns.[19] The air defense triad of medium range missiles (HAWK), short range missiles (Redeye then Stinger), and fixed wing fighters (F-4s then F/A-18s) controlled by the Marine Air Command and Control System (MACCS) formed an integrated air defense system to defend MAGTF critical assets.[20] At its peak, the Marine Corps had four Light Anti-Aircraft Missile (LAAM) HAWK Battalions and three LAAD Stinger Battalions and one stand alone Stinger battery.

Over the course of a decade most Marine Corps ground based air defense units were deactivated. The medium missile capability (HAWK) completely phased out by 1998; in exchange the U.S. Army agreed to provide that capability for the MAGTF.[21] The short range missile units rapidly deactivated starting in 2003. The first unit deactivated was the Light Armored Vehicle-Air Defense (LAV-AD) Platoon, employed to defend mobile combat units in the Marine Division. In 2004, the Marine Corps Force Structure Review Group cut two platoons from each battalion and completely deactivated the reserve battalion, Fourth LAAD Battalion.[22] In 2005 the Marine Corps divested the Avenger weapon system and replaced it with the Advance MANPAD (man-portable air defense) system. The Advance MANPAD (A-MANPAD) system consists of a High Mobility Multi-Wheeled Vehicle (HMMWV), a crew served weapon (M-2 .50 caliber machine gun or M-240B medium machine gun), and a rack capable of holding four Stinger missiles. The Avenger was costly and maintenance intensive, but possessed capabilities that the A-MANPAD did not replace, particularly a forward looking infrared (FLIR), a laser range finder, and a slue-to-cue function. In 2006, in response to no air threat in OIF or OEF and an increased demand for base defense, Headquarters Marine Corps (HQMC) officially assigned the LAAD Battalions a secondary mission to conduct ground defense of MAGTF air sites and forward operating bases when not engaged in air defense operations; something LAAD Battalions executed as an "in lieu of" mission since 2004. And finally in that same year, First Stinger Battery in Okinawa, Japan deactivated leaving only two LAAD Battalions in the Marine Corps.

The 60% reduction of LAAD Battalion structure and divesture of the Avenger occurred in anticipation of a new capability being fielded to the Marine Corps, the

Complimentary Low Altitude Weapons Systems (CLAWS). CLAWS was designed to be an expeditionary, medium range, counter to low radar cross section threats such as cruise missiles and Unmanned Aircraft Systems (UAS).[23] With a range three times that of a Stinger, it was anticipated that fewer Marines would be required to operate CLAWS for the same or increased amount of air defense coverage.[24] CLAWS successfully conducted operational testing in 2006 and appeared to be the future capability to fill the air defense gap that existed in the MAGTF.[25] However, due to fiscal limitations CLAWS was not fielded to the operational forces and remains a required, but unfunded, program in the Marine Corps. The Stinger missile, which shelf life expires in 2013, remains the only ground based air defense capability in the MAGTF.[26] The Marine Corps does not have a program to replace Stinger or CLAWS. A new materiel solution organic to a new Defense Battalion would alleviate the capability gap that currently exists in the MAGTF's ability to defend against cruise missiles and unmanned aircraft.

THE UNMANNED AIRCRAFT AND CRUISE MISSILE THREAT TO THE MAGTF

Despite the current gap in ground based air defense capabilities, the Marine Corps still needs its own ground based air defense because of the significant threat cruise missiles and unmanned aircraft will present in future conflicts. The Marine Corps has accepted risk against the air threat over the past decade and has not come under air attack despite the divesture of HAWK and reduction of Stinger. However, the air threat continues to evolve and become more lethal, easier to operate, widely proliferated, and harder to detect. To fully appreciate the severity of the threat, a study of China reveals a nation that is both striving to be a peer of the United States militarily and proliferating arms and technology throughout the world; in exchange for much needed energy, to nations such as Angola, Chad, Egypt, Indonesia, Nigeria, Central Asia, Iran, Venezuela, Russia, and Sudan.[27] China has used its enormous defense budget (estimated between $85 billion and $125 billion for 2007) to modernize its military, including producing fourth generation fighters and developing a fifth generation fighter.[28] China's emphasis on cruise missile and unmanned aircraft programs and its proliferation of weapons and technology presents future problems for the United States' military and national security.

Unmanned aircraft and cruise missiles are the fastest growing air threat to the MAGTF because they are accurate, difficult to detect, cheaper and easier to maintain than an air force, widely proliferated, and simple to employ. According to the U.S. National Air and Space Intelligence Center in 2005:

> "Proliferation of land attack cruise missiles will expand in the next decade. At least nine countries will be involved in producing these weapons. The majority of new LACMs (land attack cruise missiles) will be very accurate, conventionally armed, and available for export. The high accuracy of many LACMs will allow them to inflict serious damage on important targets, even when the missiles are armed only with conventional warheads. U.S. defense systems could be severely stressed by low-flying stealthy cruise missiles that can simultaneously attack a target from several directions."[29]

In fact, 25 countries already possess cruise missiles with a range greater than 90 miles (150 Km).[30] At least 70 countries have some form of anti-ship cruise missile, which can be altered for land attack purposes, with a little ingenuity and modification, as Iraq did with five HY-2/CSSC-3 Seersucker missiles during Operation Iraqi Freedom.[31] All five Iraqi Seersuckers successfully avoided detection and destruction by coalition forces. Distressingly, the Seersucker was built in the 1970's and is large and slow by contemporary missile standards.[32] Cruise missiles can also be employed by non-state actors, as demonstrated in 2006, when Hezbollah damaged an Israeli ship and killed four sailors with an Iranian made C-802 anti-ship missile.[33] Cruise missiles present a threat the United States military cannot defeat today with its current capabilities.

Unmanned aircraft are equally as dangerous and widespread with at least 32 countries developing over 250 different models.[34] Unmanned aircraft traditionally perform surveillance and reconnaissance missions, but in the past decade they have grown in attack capability. Disturbingly, unmanned aircraft can also be employed by non-state actors, as witnessed during the Israeli-Hezbollah war of 2006, where for the first time in a conflict, both belligerents used unmanned aircraft.[35] Unmanned aircraft and cruise missiles enable future adversaries to attack U.S. interests even when the U.S. has air superiority and therefore will continue to pose a significant threat to the MAGTF well into the future.

THE IMPORTANCE OF DETERRENCE

The U.S. military's dominance in air-to-air warfare has deterred adversaries from fighting head to head and forced them to find alternate means of attacking U.S. forces, particularly by using ballistic and cruise missiles and unmanned aircraft. In fact, enemy aircraft have not attacked Marine ground units since the battle of Okinawa in 1945.[36] The last time the U.S. faced a fix wing threat in Desert Storm, it destroyed the enemy with an air-to-air kill ratio of 41:0.[37] This fact undoubtedly deterred the Iraqi Air Force from launching a single aircraft during Operation Iraqi Freedom in 2003. The U.S. military simply has no peer competitor in the air. However, this has only driven potential adversaries into developing alternate means to attack U.S. forces as evident by a 1999 Chinese Liberation Army Daily editorial that stated, "Our military preparations need to be more directly aimed at finding tactics to exploit the weaknesses of a strong enemy."[38]

According to HQMC, "The Joint Force vision for ground based air defense is interdependent systems for all services that fight as an integrated interoperable family of systems."[39] The joint force cannot currently fulfill that vision although each service is developing programs to defeat the threat. The U.S. Army is divesting its divisional short range air defense (SHORAD) units and reorganizing them into composite air and missile defense units (Stinger/Avenger and Patriot combined) in anticipation of replacing Stinger with SLAMRAAM (surface launched advanced medium range air to air missile). SLAMRAAM (almost identical to USMC CLAWS) will undergo more operational testing in 2009 and results will determine if low-rate initial production of the system begins.[40] The Army plans to field nine total SLAMRAAM batteries, by 2013 so as not to have a gap when Stingers shelf life expires. The joint solution for cruise missile and UAS defense over land was CLAWS and SLAMRAAM in concert. With the suspension of CLAWS, nine SLAMRAAM batteries will not provide enough coverage for the entire joint force. By 2013, the Army then plans to pursue programs to further address the threat, to include a directed high energy weapon. Another U.S. Army missile, the Patriot, is capable of engaging cruise missiles and unmanned aircraft. Since Desert Storm, however, its primary mission has been ballistic missile defense. Patriot is expected to remain in service until 2025, but at $3.1 million per missile, it is not the optimal long term solution to defeat the cruise missile and UAS threat.[41]

The U.S. Navy's concept for air defense, Sea Shield, provides air defense of naval shipping in the littorals using the Aegis SPY-1 radars and SM-2 and SM-6 missiles, but will not extend far enough landward to protect the MAGTF due to over the horizon positioning of ships and the curvature of the earth. Additionally, at $3.5 million dollars per SM-6 missile, it is not a fiscally viable defense against unmanned aircraft or cruise missiles.[42] Therefore, according to HQMC, the U.S. Navy will rely on the Marine Corps to protect it from this landward threat.[43] The Marine Corps is currently assessing the way ahead for a material solution. According to Deputy Commandant for Aviation Lieutenant General G. J. Trautman's guidance, "the material solution (must) reflect the USMC ethos and be expeditionary, light weight, cost effective and austere."[44] CLAWS proved to be an effective system, but at $800,000 per AMRAAM missile it is too expensive.[45] The long term vision for the Marine Corps is a joint venture with the Army to develop a directed energy weapon to counter the cruise missile and unmanned aircraft threat, but the Marine Corps has not has not determined the interim solution.[46]

THE NEED FOR AN EXPEDITIONARY BASE DEFENSE UNIT

The MAGTF is simultaneously experiencing an increase in air threats and an increased demand for base defense. The Marine Corps has defended bases in the past, but the demand to defend expeditionary bases has reemerged in recent conflicts and will continue to be an operational requirement to support MAGTF expeditionary operations ashore in the future. According to the Marine Corps Doctrinal Publication on operations, MCDP 1-0, "Future contingencies will compel an ever increasing reliance on expeditionary bases and sites … to support and sustain expeditionary maneuver warfare."[47] MCDP 1-0 further goes on to define examples of expeditionary bases as airfields, forward operating bases, and existing facilities seized from the enemy.[48] Although MCDP 1-0 was written in 2001, it was prophetic for the considerable amount of expeditionary bases and sites used during Operations Enduring and Iraqi Freedom. The problem, however, was that until 2006, when LAAD Battalions received the secondary mission to conduct air base ground defense, a dedicated base defense unit did not exist.

In the absence of a dedicated base defense unit, the Marine Corps filled the mission in three ways; ad hoc units that received inadequate training to perform the mission (Marine Wing Support Squadrons), units that performed "in lieu of" missions (LAAD and Artillery Battalions), and units that received an official secondary mission (LAAD Battalions).[49] The assignment of a secondary mission to the LAAD Battalions has facilitated better training and equipment for the execution of a base defense mission and is a good first step to solving the problem.

The LAAD Battalions have a successful recent history of conducting base defense where no air threat was present. During Operation Enduring Freedom, a LAAD section from the Fifteenth Marine Expeditionary Unit (MEU) defended a forward arming and refueling point (FARP) at an expeditionary site in Pakistan, enabling rotary wing assets to refuel and rearm during the seizure of Camp Rhino in Afghanistan.[50] During Operation Iraqi Freedom I, Marines from Third LAAD Battalion provided ground defense for three Patriot Batteries, two forward operating bases, and four MWSS FARP teams at twenty-three different sites.[51] Since Operation Iraqi Freedom I, every LAAD unit has deployed, most multiple times, to conduct FOB security, in Iraq and Djbouti.

LAAD Battalions have conducted a variety of tasks in execution of its secondary mission to include: convoy security, combat patrols, entry control points, tactical control points, quick reaction forces, route security, watch towers, military police functions, personal security details, port security, and embassy reinforcement.[52] Since 2003, LAAD Battalions on average spend eighty percent of the available training time focused on the secondary mission and 20% on air defense.[53] The high demand for a flexible unit that can accomplish base defense missions is evident by LAAD Battalions' average 1:1 ratio of deployment to dwell time. This requirement coupled with the aforementioned cruise missile and unmanned aircraft threat exemplifies why the LAAD Battalions should be reorganized as Defense Battalions.

A NEW DEFENSE BATTALION FOR THE MAGTF

DEFENSE BATTALION ORGANIZATION

The two remaining LAAD Battalions should be reorganized and renamed Defense Battalions. Renaming is symbolic and important since the term "LAAD" is solely air defense, while "defense" based on the World War II battalions, implies air or ground defense. In order to fully define how this would work, it must be analyzed along the following areas: organization, equipment, personnel, training, and employment. First, the organization of the unit must be prepared to simultaneously accomplish both air and ground defense of expeditionary bases and critical assets. LAAD Battalion's current organization reflects the primary mission of air defense, with two firing batteries and a headquarters and service battery and is incapable of conducting both missions simultaneously. When required to conduct simultaneous missions, similar to the Defense Battalions of World War II, infantry should be tasked to support a Defense Battalion. This solution requires no additional force structure to current LAAD Battalions; instead the MAGTF Commander must direct that a habitual support relationship be established between the Wing and Division for training, evaluation, and execution of the missions.

As organized, the current LAAD Battalions do not have organic radars to detect an air threat. Instead, LAAD Battalions rely on early warning and cueing over a data link from radars organic to the MACCS. In order to detect and engage cruise missiles and unmanned aircraft, a Defense Battalion would require an organic surveillance platoon similar to the organization of original Defense Battalions. This surveillance platoon would come from the Marine Air Control Squadron (MACS) as structure reorganization to support the fielding of the new Ground/Air Task Organized Radars (GATOR).

Although potential exists for a Defense Battalion to conduct missions not associated with an aircraft wing, it should remain as a subordinate unit to the Marine Air Control Group (MACG), within the Marine Aircraft Wing for two reasons. First, the control of aircraft and missiles and anti-air warfare are functions of Marine aviation that require detailed coordination and integration to successfully execute. The MACG plans for, and integrates these two functions. Secondly, in order to employ forward based aviation assets, the Marine Aircraft Wing requires a dedicated force to defend expeditionary air sites ranging from forward arming and refueling points to main air bases.

DEFENSE BATTALION PERSONNEL

A new Defense Battalion would require minimal personnel additions. Currently, LAAD Battalions are organized to accomplish an air defense mission for the MAGTF, with the manpower to reflect that mission. Since the addition of the secondary mission, LAAD Battalions have not received any additional manpower. According to command chronologies of Second LAAD Battalion and Third LAAD Battalion, since 2003 the average manpower of a battalion has consisted of 22 Officers and 300 enlisted, while the average base defense mission, according to a survey of LAAD personnel, has required between 500 and 800 Marines.[54] LAAD's additional required manpower has been filled

13

by individual augments from within the Wing. This is a sufficient solution for a relatively benign environment; assuming the augments attach in time to go through the pre-deployment training program. When the threat dictates that a more capable force is needed, the infantry unit with a habitual support relationship should attach a task organized force to the Defense Battalion. The challenges associated with attaching an infantry unit to a Defense Battalion will be worked out in an annual evaluated joint exercise. To help facilitate and train for the tasks associated with the secondary mission the following personnel should also be added to the table of organization for a new Defense Battalion: one 0302 infantry officer, one 0369 infantry staff non-commissioned officer (SNCO), and one 5811 military police SNCO. The surveillance platoon would also require additional personnel and consist of Air Defense Control Officers (Military Occupational Specialty 7210), Air Defense Controllers (7234s/36s), and Aviation Radar Repairers and Technicians (5942/48).

DEFENSE BATTALION EQUIPMENT

The materiel solution for a Defense Battalion must be flexible, inexpensive, expeditionary, multi-use, and counter the cruise missile and unmanned air threat. The high cost of missiles currently makes it fiscally unfeasible for the Marine Corps to purchase a missile to counter the threat. The Department of Defense Advance Research Projects Agency (DARPA) is working on a $40,000 missile that could intercept cruise missiles, however most missile system options range from $300,000 (multi-mission missile) to $800,000 (AMRAAM on CLAWS) per missile.[55]

The Stinger missile is the cheapest, at approximately $50,000 a missile, and is currently being upgraded by its developer Raytheon with a proximity fuse to improve its lethality against unmanned aircraft. According to a Raytheon spokesperson, "By adding a proximity fuse to that (Stinger) it's a very cost effective way to enhance lethality without having to buy a new missile or even develop a new missile."[56] Despite the improved capability of the Stinger, the limiting factor for engaging cruise missiles and unmanned aircraft is the Stinger gunner's ability to visually acquire the target, a challenge further exacerbated by low observable threats. For this reason, the Stinger missile, although technically capable of engaging a cruise missile or UAS, is not the Marine Corps' solution to the threat. Stinger teams do not have an ability to shoot on the move, "slue-to-cue" from an early warning or fire control radar, or with the current thermal night sight, effectively identify targets at night. The Stinger's shelf life expires in 2013 and a replacement is desperately needed.

Perhaps the most economical and effective weapon to defeat the threat is an anti-aircraft artillery (AAA) radar guided-gun with a high rate of fire. In fact, during Operation Allied Force, Serbian AAA or machine guns as small as 7.62mm shot down the majority of the 21 NATO unmanned aircraft lost during combat.[57] The U.S. Navy uses an anti-air gun, the MK 15 Phalanx Close-In Weapons System (CIWS or "sea-whiz"), to defend ships against anti-ship cruise missiles.[58] The system has utility on the ground as well. Since 2005, the U.S. Army started employing a ground version of the Phalanx as part of a weapon system called C-RAM (counter rocket, artillery, and mortar) to defend FOBs in Iraq against the rocket and mortar threat. C-RAM consists of a 20mm Gatling gun, a self contained search and track radar, and tracer rounds that detonate upon contact or when the tracer extinguishes.[59] C-RAM is so successful that Israel may buy the system to defend against the rocket threat they face.[60] However, C-RAM, with a cost of $15 million per system, is not a viable solution for the Marine Corps.[61] In addition to the cost, C-RAM employs off of the back of a tractor trailer, vice a HMMWV, and therefore does not meet Marine Corps expeditionary standards. The materiel solution does not currently exist, but a radar guided machine gun with a high rate of fire has proven its ability to engage the threat and utility to perform other missions when not engaged in air defense missions. For example, during Operation Just Cause in Panama, one U.S. Army AAA Vulcan platoon caused 10% of all the enemy casualties.[62]

As proven on Wake Island during World War II, Defense Battalions require organic radars to detect the air threat. The Marine Corps' future radar, the GATOR, is exactly what a Defense Battalion needs. GATOR can detect cruise missiles, unmanned aircraft, fixed and rotary wing aircraft, and future increments will even include a counter-battery fire detection capability. In March, 2007, production started on the first 15 GATORs, dedicated for short range air defense and air surveillance.[63] These GATOR radars should serve as the organic radar for a Defense Battalion.

DEFENSE BATTALION EMPLOYMENT

Defense Battalions of World War II proved their merit in their ability to adjust to meet the tasks of the mission at hand, whether defending an advance naval base, conducting combat patrols, or providing fire support for an amphibious assault. A new Defense Battalion must be no different. A Defense Battalion could defend MAGTF critical assets from an air or ground threat and would be able to support all sizes of MAGTFs, from a MEU to a MEF. The level of Defense Battalion support for each MAGTF would be task organized and scalable for the anticipated mission, but would consist of air defense, surveillance, maintenance and support elements, and a command element. When the threat dictates that simultaneous air and ground defense of an asset is required, task organized infantry should be attached to the unit. When no air threat exists, the Defense Battalion would be employed as strictly ground defense.

Defense Battalions could be employed to defend other assets within the MAGTF to include command and control nodes, assembly areas, logistical support bases, maneuver units, key terrain features and chokepoints, population centers, lines of communication, and maritime prepositioned force (MPF) offload sites; all static sites with the exception of maneuver units. Maneuver units are mobile, tactically dispersed on the battlefield, and typically not a high payoff target for an enemy to engage with a costly weapon. It is therefore unlikely that maneuver units will be targeted by cruise missiles. However, the opposite is true of unmanned aircraft. Maneuver units are the most likely to encounter enemy unmanned aircraft on the battlefield due to the close proximity to the enemy on the forward edge of the battle area and the relatively short distance unmanned aircraft can be employed from a ground control station. The MAGTF Commander ultimately determines the air and ground defense priorities based on enemy threat capability and each asset's criticality, vulnerability, and recoverability.

Flexibility and multi-mission capabilities will allow Defense Battalions to be employed in a variety of ways. The Defense Battalion could be employed in general support of the MAGTF, direct support of an element of the MAGTF, attached to another unit, or even employed as a maneuver unit. Similar to Defense Battalions in World War II, employing a Defense Battalion as a maneuver unit would provide the MAGTF Commander with a heavily armed, well trained unit that could free an infantry battalion to conduct other missions.

DEFENSE BATTALION TRAINING

From 1998 to 2003, LAAD Battalions conducted an average of fifteen air defense exercises a year ranging from small platoon exercises to larger battery and battalion exercises, integrated with the MACCS and the ground combat element's scheme of maneuver.[64] Over the past decade, 15% of a battalion's combat strength was attached to a Marine Expeditionary Unit.[65] Since 2003, Second and Third LAAD Battalion each deployed four times to perform a base defense mission. The limited dwell time between deployments forced battalion commanders to prioritize the secondary mission as the focus of effort for training. For the past 5 years, 80% of LAAD Battalions' training has focused on base defense tasks in preparation for the next deployment.[66] During that same period the average number of air defense exercises conducted in a battalion dropped down to two.[67] It is no wonder the air defense skill sets in the two LAAD Battalions have atrophied to the point where some LAAD officers and staff non-commissioned officers believe their unit is no longer capable of conducting an air defense mission.[68] The data clearly highlights that under the current construct a LAAD Battalion is only able to train to a proficient level on one mission at a time.

In order to ensure that a Defense Battalion maintains at least one battery suitably trained to execute ground or air defense it should split its training focus between the two subordinate batteries. For example, Battery A would focus 80% of its allotted training schedule on air defense and 20% on ground defense, while Battery B would spend 80% on ground defense and 20% on air defense. When a battalion receives a deployment order, a mission analysis must be conducted to conclude if air and ground defense is required and determine the associated level of training effort for each mission.

Additionally, to establish a habitual working relationship, a Defense Battalion and an infantry battalion should jointly conduct one command post exercise and one evaluated base defense exercise per year to effectively integrate an attached infantry unit, should the need arise.

A Defense Battalion could be assigned its own battle-space to operate in if employed as a maneuver unit or when defending a base. In recent operations, LAAD Battalions were assigned an area extending 20 kilometers from the base. Unlike infantry units that are assigned battle-space, LAAD Battalions do not possess any tactical air control parties or fire support coordinators. Currently, LAAD Battalions conducting base defense missions lack any indirect fire capability above an M-203 grenade launcher and trained personnel to call for indirect fire. LAAD Battalion Marines are also not trained to terminally control aviation fires or control a landing zone. Therefore, a Defense Battalion should either receive training to control fires and aircraft within its assigned area of operations or be supported by trained and qualified observers and Joint Terminal Attack Controllers from the Division when required.

CONCLUSION

The Marine Corps should convert LAAD Battalions to Defense Battalions to provide air defense and base defense for the MAGTF. During World War II, Defense Battalions' success depended on their flexibility, multi-use weapons, cross training, and task organizing. A new Defense Battalion, based on the World War II model, is the solution to two problems facing the MAGTF; the cruise missile and UAS threat and the increased demand for base defense units. New Defense Battalions, formed by using existing LAAD Battalions as the foundation, would provide a well trained, dedicated unit to the defense mission. The habitual training relationship established with an infantry unit would enable both air and ground defense missions to be conducted simultaneously. When only one mission is required, the Defense Battalion would conduct it. The task organized force structure, multi-purpose weapons, and cross training would make a Defense Battalion a versatile unit with several employment options.

The rapidly increasing cruise missile and unmanned aircraft threat requires the Marine Corps to maintain an organic capability to defend itself. The threat is currently proliferating faster than systems to counter it. Cruise missiles and unmanned aircraft will continue their proliferation throughout the world well into the future as developing countries like China look for asymmetric ways to attack a superior force that places so much emphasis on achieving air superiority. Additionally, as U.S. forces continue their involvement in irregular warfare, the usage of unmanned aircraft and cruise missiles by non-state actors will also pose an increased threat to the MAGTF.

The MAGTF will continue to need units to defend expeditionary sites from ground attack for the foreseeable future. Defense Battalions present the ideal solution for a unit that is well trained, well equipped, properly manned, and organized to accomplish a base defense mission. The equipment solution must be expeditionary, affordable, and flexible enough to support both missions. An anti-aircraft artillery gun with fire control radar and a high rate of fire presents the best option. As in World War II, Defense Battalions must also have organic surveillance radars to detect and defeat the threat.

A new Defense Battalion would be prepared to provide air and ground defense of MAGTF critical assets. The cost to make the change is minimal, but the cost of not making the change could prove to be fatal for the MAGTF in future conflicts.

Notes

[1]David J. Ulbrich, *Thomas Holcomb and the Advent of the Marine Corps Defense Battalion 1936-1941*, (Occasional paper, History and museums division Marine Corps University, 2004), 41.

[2]Charles D. Melson, *Condition Red: Marine Defense Battalions in World War II* (Pamphlet in the Marines in World War II commemorative series, 1996), 2.

[3]Ulbrich, 17.

[4]Ibid, 17.

[5]Melson, 3.

[6]Ulbrich, 38.

[7]Melson, 1.

[8]Ibid, 4.

[9]Ibid, 4.

[10]Ibid, 4.

[11]Ibid, 6.

[12]Ulbrich, 38.

[13]Melson, 6.

[14]Ibid, 13.

[15]Ibid, 10.

[16]Lucas T. Cuccia II, "Evolution of Mission: The Transformation of Marine Defense Battalions in the Second World War," (M.A. Thesis, University of New Orleans, December 2004), 20.

[17]Melson, 15, 24.

[18]Ibid, 15.

[19]Mark A. King, "The Hunt For Adequate Protection: Ground-Based Air Defense In the USMC," (masters thesis, Marine Corps University, 1995).

[20] Ibid.

[21] Craig R. Doty, Headquarters U.S. Marine Corps, information paper, "Status of Marine Corps Ground Based Air Defense, GBADs Evolving Role in the Marine Corps," June 2008.

[22] Ibid.

[23] Ibid.

[24] Ibid.

[25] Author's experience.

[26] Doty.

[27] White House, Annual report to congress, *Military Power of the People's Republic of China 2007* (Washington, DC: GPO, 2008) 9, 10.

[28] Ibid, 25, 28.

[29] Andrew Feickert, *Cruise Missile Proliferation*. CRS Report for Congress RS21252. (Washington, DC: Congressional Research Service, July 28, 2005), 2.

[30] Andrew Feickert, *Missile Survey: Ballistic and cruise missiles of selected foreign countries*. CRS Report for Congress RL30427. (Washington, DC: Congressional Research Service, July 26, 2005), 2.

[31] Ibid, 24.

[32] Ibid, 24.

[33] Matt Matthews, *We were caught unprepared : the 2006 Hezbollah-Israeli War* (Ft Leavenworth, KS: Combat Studies Institute Press, 2008), 19.

[34] Joseph A. Christoff, U.S. Congress. House. Testimony before the Committee on Government Reform, Subcommittee on National Security, Emerging Threats, and International Relations. *Nonproliferation Improvements Needed for Controls on Exports of Cruise Missile and Unmanned Aerial Vehicle Technology*, March 9, 2004.

[35] Lieutenant General (Ret.) James C. Riley and Brigadier General (Ret.) Michael Means, "The Looming Force Protection Crisis for Brigade Combat Teams," *Air Defense Artillery*, (Oct-December 2006), 9-11.

[36] King.

[37]Chad E. Montgomery, "Where was LAAD?" Expeditionary Warfare School Contemporary Issue Paper, Quantico, Virginia, 2004.

[38]White House, Annual report to congress, *Military Power of the People's Republic of China 2007* (Washington, DC: GPO, 2008) 13.

[39]Doty.

[40]Kate Brannen, "Raytheon: SLAMRAAM Successfully Completes Integration Training," *Inside Defense,* (8/4/2008), http://www.insidedefense.com/secure/display.asp?docnum=ARMY-20-31-12&f=defense_2002.ask (accessed Jan 20, 2008).

[41]Doty.

[42]Doty.

[43]Ibid.

[44]Craig R. Doty, Headquarters U.S. Marine Corps, information paper, "Status of Marine Corps Ground Based Air Defense, Courses of Action for USMC GBAD," June 2008.

[45]Ibid.

[46]Ibid.

[47]Headquarters U.S. Marine Corps, Marine Corps Operations, MCDP 1-0 (Washington, DC: U.S. Marine Corps, September 27, 2001) pg 2-18.

[48]Ibid, pg 2-18.

[49]Author's experience.

[50]Ibid.

[51]Ibid.

[52]LAAD questionnaire developed by author.

[53]Ibid.

[54] 2nd LAAD Battalion and 3rd LAAD Battalion Command Chronologies 1998-2006.

[55] Doty, GBAD COAs and
Christopher Bolkcom and Ravi R. Hichkad. *Cruise Missile Defense*. CRS Report for Congress RS21921. (Washington, DC: Congressional Research Service, May 2, 2005), 6.

[56] "Raytheon Develops Concept To Modify Stingers For UAV Threat." Helicopter News 34.24 (Nov 25, 2008): NA. Military and Intelligence Collection. Gale. GRAY RESEARCH CENTER (C40RCL). 18 Jan. 2009 <http://find.galegroup.com/ips/start.do?prodId=IPS>.

[57] Tim Ripley, "UAV's over Kosovo – did the earth move?" *Defense Systems Daily* (December 1, 1999) http://www.defence-data.com/features/fpage34.htm (Accessed Jan 11, 2009).

[58] John Pike, "MK 15 Phalanx Close-In Weapons System (CIWS)," Federation of American Scientists http://www.fas.org/man/dod-101/sys/ship/weaps/mk-15.htm (accessed Jan 11, 2009).

[59] Ibid.

[60] Yaakov Katz and jpost.com staff, "Israel May Buy Rapid-Fire Cannon," *The Jerusalem Post online edition*, Dec. 20, 2007, http://www.jpost.com/servlet/Satellite?cid=1196847389509&pagename=JPost%2FJPArticle%2FPrinter (Accessed Jan 11, 2009).

[61] Ibid.

[62] http://www.globalsecurity.org/military/agency/army/ada.htm (Accessed Jan 15, 2009).

[63] http://www.defense-update.com/products/g/GATOR.htm *Defense Update* (Accessed Jan 15, 2009).

[64] 2nd and 3rd LAAD Battalion Command Chronologies 1998-2006.

[65] Ibid.

[66] LAAD questionnaire developed by author.

[67] 2nd and 3rd LAAD Battalion Command Chronologies 1998-2006.

[68] LAAD questionnaire developed by author.

Bibliography

Albiero, Lou Major, Operations Officer, 2d LAAD Bn, LAAD Questionnaire from
    Author.

Bolkcom, Christopher and Ravi R. Hichkad. *Cruise Missile Defense.* CRS Report for
    Congress RS21921. Washington, DC: Congressional Research Service, May 2,
    2005.

Brannen, Kate, Army and Boeing Plan to Test "Warrior Shield" Counter-UAV
    Capability," *Inside Defense,* November 5, 2008.
    http://www.insidedefense.com/secure/display.asp?docnum=MISSILE-14-23-
    11&f=defense_2002.ask (Accessed Jan 11, 2009).

Brannen, Kate "Raytheon: SLAMRAAM Successfully Completes Integration Training,"
    Inside Defense, (8/4/2008).
    http://www.insidedefense.com/secure/display.asp?docnum=ARMY-20-31-
    12&f=defense_2002.ask (accessed Jan 20, 2008).

Bruntlett, J. "Advanced Naval Bases - Necessary And Dependable?" Master's thesis,
    The Marine Corps Command and Staff College, Quantico, Virginia, 1984.

Crim, Chris Major, Operations Officer, 3d LAAD Bn, LAAD Questionnaire from
    Author.

Christoff, Joseph A. U.S. Congress. House. Testimony before the Committee on
    Government Reform, Subcommittee on National Security, Emerging Threats, and
    International Relations. *Nonproliferation Improvements Needed for Controls on
    Exports of Cruise Missile and Unmanned Aerial Vehicle Technology,* March 9,
    2004.

Commission on U.S.-China Economic and Security Review. *Report to Congress.*
    Washington, DC: Government Printing Office, 2008.

"Cruise missile threat soaring, so U.S. urgently needs cruise missile defense." Space and
    Missile Defense Report 8.27 (July 16, 2007): 3(1). Military and Intelligence
    Collection. Gale. GRAY RESEARCH CENTER (C40RCL). 29 Dec. 2008.

Cuccia II, Lucas T. "Evolution of Mission: The Transformation of Marine Defense
    Battalions in the Second World War." Master's thesis, University of New
    Orleans, 2004.

Doty, Craig R., Headquarters U.S. Marine Corps, information paper, "Status of Marine
    Corps Ground Based Air Defense, Courses of Action for USMC GBAD," June
    2008.

25

Doty, Craig R., Headquarters U.S. Marine Corps, information paper, "Status of Marine Corps Ground Based Air Defense, GBADs Evolving Role in the Marine Corps," June 2008.

Doty, Craig R., Headquarters U.S. Marine Corps, information paper, "Status of Marine Corps Ground Based Air Defense, USMC GBAD Requirements & US Army and US Navy Strategies," June 2008.

Grimmett, Richard F. *Conventional arms transfers to developing nations*. CRS report for congress RL34723, Washington, DC: Congressional Research Service, Oct 23, 2008.

Feickert, Andrew. *Missile Survey: Ballistic and cruise missiles of selected foreign countries*. CRS Report for Congress RL30427. Washington, DC: Congressional Research Service, July 26, 2005.

Feickert, Andrew. *Cruise Missile Proliferation*. CRS Report for Congress RS21252. Washington, DC: Congressional Research Service, July 28, 2005.

Field Manual Headquarters. Army Theater Missile Defense Operations. FM 100-12. Washington DC: Headquarters U.S Army, March 31, 2000.

Gruben, SSgt Air Base Ground Defense Chief, MAWTS-1, LAAD Questionnaire from Author.

Harris, MSgt Ira GBAD Division Chief, MAWTS-1, LAAD Questionnaire from Author.

Headquarters U.S. Marine Corps. Marine Corps Operations. MCDP 1-0. Washington, DC: Headquarters U.S. Marine Corps, September 27, 2001.

Hoyle, Craig "UK MoD reveals UAV losses in Iraq, Afghanistan" *Flight International* 06/06/07.

Katz, Yaakov and jpost.com staff, "Israel May Buy Rapid-Fire Cannon," *The Jerusalem Post online edition,* Dec. 20, 2007. http://www.jpost.com/servlet/Satellite?cid=1196847389509&pagename=JPost%2 FJPArticle%2FPrinter (Accessed Jan 11, 2009).

Kan, Shirley A., *China and proliferation of weapons of mass destruction and missiles: Policy issues*. CRS report for congress RL31555, Washington, DC: Congressional Research Service, March 6, 2008.

King, Mark A. "The Hunt for Adequate Protection: Ground-Based Air Defense in the USMC." Master's thesis, The Marine Corps Command and Staff College, Quantico, Virgina, 1995.

Krauss, Marcus Capt, GBAD Division Head, MAWTS-1, LAAD Questionnaire from
    Author.

"Land Attack Cruise Missiles," globalsecurity.org
    http://www.globalsecurity.org/wmd/world/china/lacm.htm (accessed Jan 5, 2009).

Leal, MSgt William, Operations Chief, 3d LAAD Bn, LAAD Questionnaire from Author.

Maynard, Stephen R. "Marine Defense Battalions, October 1939 – December 1942:
    Their Contributions in the early phases of World War II." Master's thesis,
    University of North Texas, 1996.

Means, Brigadier General (Ret.) Michael and Lieutenant General (Ret.) James C. Riley.
    "The Looming Force Protection Crisis for Brigade Combat Teams." *Air Defense
    Artillery*, (Oct-December 2006): 9-11.

Melson, Charles D. "Condition Red: Marine Defense Battalions in World War II."
    Marines in World War II Commemorative Series pamphlet, History and Museums
    Division, HQMC, Washington D.C., 1996.

Miasnikov, Eugene, "Threat of Terrorism Using Unmanned Aerial Vehicles: Technical
    Aspects", Center for Arms Control, Energy and Environmental Studies at MIPT,
    Dolgoprudny, June 2004, 26.

Montgomery, Chad E. "Where was LAAD?" Expeditionary Warfare School
    Contemporary Issue Paper, Quantico, Virginia, 2004.

Pike, John "MK 15 Phalanx Close-In Weapons System (CIWS)," Federation of American
    Scientists
    http://www.fas.org/man/dod-101/sys/ship/weaps/mk-15.htm (accessed Jan 11,
    2009).

"Raytheon Develops Concept To Modify Stingers For UAV Threat." Helicopter
    News 34.24 (Nov 25, 2008): NA. Military and Intelligence
    Collection. Gale. GRAY RESEARCH CENTER (C40RCL). 18 Jan. 2009
    <http://find.galegroup.com/ips/start.do?prodId=IPS>.

Ripley, Tim "UAV's over Kosovo – did the earth move?" *Defense Systems Daily*
    (December 1, 1999).
    http://www.defence-data.com/features/fpage34.htm (Accessed Jan 11, 2009).

Seelig, Frederick A. *One Marine Mustang's Memoirs: Fifty Months with Defense
    Battalions in the Pacific, 1940-1945*, Edited by Marvin L. Brown. New York,
    NY: Vantage Press, 1997.

Ulbrich, David J. "Thomas Holcomb and the Advent of the Marine Corps Defense Battalion 1936-1941." Occasional paper, History and Museums Division, Marine Corps University, 2004.

"Unmanned Aerial Vehicles," globalsecurity.org http://www.globalsecurity.org/military/world/china/uav.htm (accessed Jan 5, 2009).

U.S. Department of the Army. *U.S. Army 2008 Modernization Strategy*, Office of the Deputy Chief of Staff G-8, Washington, DC: Department of Defense, 25 July 2008.

U.S Department of Defense. *Quadrennial Defense Review Report*, submitted by Donald Rumsfeld. Arlington, VA: Department of Defense, February 6, 2006.

U.S. Joint Forces Command. *The Joint Operating Evironment, Challenges and Implications for the Future Joint Force*, Suffolk, VA: Department of Defense, November 25, 2008.

Van Diepen, Vann. *Cruise Missiles and Unmanned Air Vehicles*, Testimony Before the Senate Governmental Affairs Subcommittee on International Security, Proliferation, and Federal Services, Washington, DC June 11, 2002.

White House, Annual report to congress, *Military Power of the People's Republic of China 2007* (Washington, DC: GPO, 2008) 1-48.

Zuber, Wayne Major, former Operations Officer, 3d LAAD Bn, LAAD Questionnaire from author.

2nd LAAD Bn command chronologies from 1998 to 2006.

3rd LAAD Bn command chronologies from 1998 to 2005.